Australia

by Shirley W. Gray

Content Adviser: Professor Sherry L. Field,
Department of Social Science Education, College of Education,
The University of Georgia

Reading Adviser: Dr. Linda D. Labbo,
Department of Reading Education, College of Education,
The University of Georgia

COMPASS POINT BOOKS

Minneapolis, Minnesota

FIRST REPORTS

Compass Point Books
151 Good Counsel Drive
Mankato, MN 56002-0669
877-845-8392
www.capstonepub.com

Photographs ©: David Austen/FPG International, cover; Photri-Microstock, 4; Index Stock Imagery, 6; Photri-Microstock/Prenzel, 7 top; Unicorn Stock Photos/Charles E. Schmidt, 7 bottom; Dave Watts/Tom Stack and Associates, 8; James P. Rowan, 9; Photo Network/Chad Ehlers, 10; Trip/Eric Smith, 11, 12, 13, 14; Dave Watts/Tom Stack and Associates, 15; Index Stock Imagery, 16; North Wind Pictures Archive, 17 top; Photo Network/Darrell Jones, 17 bottom; Travelpix/FPG International, 18; International Stock/Johan Elbers, 19; Photri-Microstock, 20; Visuals Unlimited/J. Alock, 21; Reuters/David Gray/Archive Photos, 22; Archive Photos, 24; North Wind Picture Archive, 25; James P. Rowan, 26; Stock Montage, 27 top; Terry Qing/FPG International, 27 bottom; Unicorn Stock Photos/Marshall R. Prescott, 28; Photo Network/Chad Ehlers, 29; Index Stock Imagery, 30, 31; Dave Watts/Tom Stack and Associates, 32 top; Trip/Eric Smith, 32 bottom; Photri-Microstock/Prenzel, 34; International Stock/Auschromes, 35; Visuals Unlimited/Tom J. Ulrich, 36; Photri-Microstock, 37; Photo Network/Paul Thompson, 38; Visuals Unlimited/Jon Bertsch, 39; Dave Fleetham/Tom Stack and Associates, 40; Trip/Eric Smith, 41; Dave Watts/Tom Stack and Associates, 42; Unicorn Stock Photos/Marie Mills/David Cummings, 45.

Editors: E. Russell Primm and Emily J. Dolbear
Photo Researcher: Svetlana Zhurkina
Photo Selector: Dawn Friedman
Design: Bradfordesign, Inc.
Cartography: XNR Productions, Inc.

Library of Congress Cataloging-in-Publication Data
Gray, Shirley W.
   Australia / by Shirley W. Gray.
     p. cm. — (First reports)
   Includes bibliographical references and index.
   Summary: An introduction to the geography, history, culture, and people of Australia.
   ISBN 978-0-7565-0026-9 (library binding)
   ISBN 978-0-7565-1199-9 (paperback)
    1. Australia—Juvenile literature. [1. Australia.] I. Title. II. Series.
   DU96 .G735 2000
   994—dc21
                                                       00-008523

Printed in the United States of America in Stevens Point, Wisconsin.
072013   007414R

Table of Contents

The Land Down Under

"G'd-day, mate. Welcome to Australia!"

You might hear this greeting if you visit Australia. Australia lies south of the **equator** in the southern half of the world. Americans call it the land "down under"

▲ *An Australian sheepherder on his motorcycle*

▲ *Map of Australia*

because it is located "down under" the equator. In fact, the word *Australia* comes from the Latin word *australis*, which means "southern."

▲ *A view of Australia from space*

Australia is the sixth-largest country in the world. And it is the only country that is also a **continent**. A continent is one of Earth's seven great landmasses. Australia also includes the island of Tasmania. This island lies 130 miles (209 kilometers) off the southeast coast of Australia.

▲ *Hobart, the capital of Tasmania*

Australia is made up of six states and two territories. Canberra is its capital city. Canberra is in southern Australia.

▲ *Parliament House in Canberra*

Australia's Land

▲ *The plains of New South Wales*

Australia has several types of land. It has flat land called **plains**. It has **plateaus**, high flat areas with steep sides. Another striking feature of this enormous

▲ *Blue Mountains National Park in the mountainous eastern part of Australia*

landmass is its mountains. Australia's most mountainous land lies along the east coast.

Oceans and seas surround Australia. Most of the people in Australia live in eastern Australia near the South Pacific Ocean. Sydney is the largest city in Australia. It is on the east coast of Australia. The city

▲ *The famous Opera House in front of Sydney's skyline*

of Melbourne is the second-largest city in Australia. It stands on the southeast coast.

A long stretch of mountains called the Great Dividing Range separates eastern Australia from the middle of the country. The highest of these mountains are the Australian Alps. People like to ski here.

▲ *Skiing in the Australian Alps*

Salt Lakes

▲ *A salt lake in South Australia*

Most of Australia's natural lakes are salty. During the dry season, these lakes are just dry beds of salt. Fortunately, farmers and ranchers have found a way to get freshwater. They drill deep wells to bring this water to the surface. Dams trap the water and create large pools. Farmers and ranchers then use the water in these pools for their sheep and cattle.

▲ *Sheep graze near water dams in eastern Australia.*

Deep in the ground, pools of water are trapped within the rock. The largest of these pools is the Great Artesian Basin. In some places, the water bubbles to the surface in natural springs.

◄ *A hot water well in the Great Artesian Basin*

The Outback

▲ *Sand dunes in the state called South Australia*

The center of Australia is called the **outback**. It got its
name because it is "out back" of the mountains of
the Great Dividing Range. The outback has three
deserts and several small mountain areas. Few people

▲ *There are few houses and farms on outback roads.*

live in the outback because it is dry, rugged land and hard to reach.

Not many people lived in the outback until gold was discovered in 1851. Then many people rushed to the state of New South Wales hoping to make their fortune. A few years later, a larger gold field was found in the state of Victoria. Today the town of Kalgoorlie is the center of this gold-mining district.

▲ *A riverbed claim during Australia's gold rush*

▲ *There are many gold mines in Kalgoorlie.*

▲ *Ayers Rock, or Uluru, in the Northern Territory*

The dry desert winds of the outback have carved large rocks into unusual shapes. One of these is Ayers Rock in the Northern Territory. The native people call it *Uluru*. It is the largest rock in the world.

The Aboriginal People

The first people to live in Australia were the **Aborigines**. Scientists think they came to Australia from Southeast Asia about 40,000 years ago.

Aborigines learned to live in this new land. They invented the **boomerang** to help them hunt birds and

▲ *An Aborigine prepares to throw two boomerangs.*

▲ *Dingoes are wild dogs that may have helped the Aborigines hunt.*

other small animals. The boomerang is a curved
wooden stick that comes back to the thrower.
Boomerangs are used today for fun or sport. The
Aborigines may have also used the **dingo**, a wild dog,
for hunting.

The early Aborigines were also artists and musi-
cians. They painted detailed designs on rocks and
tree bark. Music was also an important part of their

▲ A painting of an Aborigine figure throwing a boomerang

▲ *An Aboriginal man plays a didjeridoo between sacred wooden spirit sculptures.*

lives. Some Aborigines played the didjeridoo, a trumpet made from a long, hollow tree branch. The didjeridoo is still a popular instrument today.

Many Aborigines died of diseases brought by the Europeans. Others died in war. And many died of harsh mistreatment by European settlers in the 1700s and 1800s. Thousands of Aborigines were forced to leave their hunting grounds. A 1967 law returned some land to the Aboriginal people.

European Explorers and Settlements

The first explorers from Portugal, Spain, and the Netherlands arrived in Australia in the 1600s. Although these countries sent explorers to Australia, they did not send settlers to build any permanent settlements.

English explorers also visited Australia. In 1770, Captain James Cook landed at Botany Bay on the east coast. He encouraged other people from Britain to settle in this new country.

Several years later, the British

▲ Captain James Cook

▲ *A view of Sydney's harbor in the 1850s*

government decided to make Australia a prison colony. In 1788, Captain Arthur Phillip brought more than 700 prisoners to Australia. They formed the first British settlement. Over time, the settlement became the city of Sydney. The British government continued to send prisoners to Australia until about 1850.

▲ The ruins of a prison in Tasmania, where the British sent prisoners

When the prisoners had served their sentence, they were free. Many were given land. They got a new start.

These settlers soon learned that farming was difficult in Australia. However, the soil was good for grass and animals that graze. The settlers began raising sheep on the central plains. They sold the wool to

▲ Early settlers raised sheep for their wool.

▼ A modern sheep ranch in Australia

Britain. Sweaters and blankets made from Australian wool are still extremely popular around the world today.

Australia Today

▲ *Australians value their country's history, independence, and natural beauty.*

Australia became an independent country in 1901. It still has ties to Britain. The king or queen of Great Britain is the head of state in Australia, but has no real power. The prime minister is in charge of the government. The prime minister is elected by the people of Australia.

More than 18 million people live in Australia today. The state of Queensland is the fastest-growing area. Many people are drawn to its beautiful beaches and warm weather.

Because Australia is south of the equator, its seasons are the opposite of those in areas north of the equator. In Australia, June and July are winter months, with a temperature of about 50° Fahrenheit (10° Celsius). January and February are summer

▲ *Beachgoers flock to Sydney's famous Bondi Beach.*

months with a temperature of about 70° Fahrenheit (21° Celsius).

Children in Australia usually go to school all year round. At lunch, they might eat lamb or vegemite sandwiches. Vegemite is a spread made from yeast and vegetables. It is as popular in Australia as peanut butter is in North America. Children like to play soccer, a British game called cricket, and netball, a game similar to basketball.

▲ *Australian schoolchildren eating lunch*

Life in the Outback

In the outback, many people live and work on sheep and cattle ranches. More sheep are raised in Australia than in any other country. But the wild dogs called dingoes are a prob-lem. A single dingo can kill fifty sheep in one night. So ranchers built the world's largest fence to keep their sheep safe. The Dog Fence is more than 3,300 miles (5,310 kilo-meters) long.

Life in the outback is hard. The towns are often hundreds of miles apart. People

▲ An isolated sheep ranch in the outback of New South Wales

▲ The Dog Fence at the border of New South Wales and South Australia

▼ Doctors from the Royal Flying Doctor Service help a patient into their plane.

living on a ranch have trouble getting to a doctor if they are sick or hurt. However, the Royal Flying Doctor Service brings doctors, nurses, and dentists to these areas by plane.

Children cannot travel to schools in the outback either. Many students do their schoolwork at home and mail it to teachers in town. The *Schools of the Air* program lets the children talk to their teachers over the radio. Teachers also use the Internet to teach children living in the outback.

Unusual Animals

Australia may be best known to the rest of the world for its many unusual animals. Some of these animals are found nowhere else on Earth.

▲ *A koala with her baby*

Many of Australia's strangest and most popular animals are **marsupials**. Marsupials carry their young in a pouch on their stomach. The koala is a marsupial, for example.

Koalas look like furry, cuddly teddy bears. They sleep during the day and eat at night. Koalas eat mainly the leaves of eucalyptus trees. Eucalyptus trees are large, hardwood trees found in forests of eastern Australia. Many of these forests are being cut down to make more room for people. That means less food for koalas.

The kangaroo is one of Australia's national symbols. It is a marsupial too. The great gray kangaroo can jump 6 feet (2 meters) in one leap. The wallaby is a small kangaroo.

▲ *A kangaroo carries a joey, or young kangaroo, in her pouch.*

Kangaroos eat grass and bushes, just like cattle and sheep. Some ranchers think kangaroos are pests because they take food from cattle and sheep.

The Tasmanian devil is a marsupial found only in Tasmania. Prowling at night, this powerful meat-eater eats the bodies of dead animals. It also hunts live animals, such as wallabies or opossums.

▲ *Tasmanian devils feed.*

The emu is another national symbol. Emus are large birds that cannot fly. An adult emu stands up to 6 feet (180 centimeters) tall and can run as fast as 30 miles (48 kilometers) an hour. The female emu lays the eggs. The male sits on the nest until the eggs hatch.

▲ *The emu is a bird, but it cannot fly.*

The Great Barrier Reef

▲ *Part of the Great Barrier Reef near Port Douglas in Queensland*

Australia is also famous for its sea creatures. The
Great Barrier Reef is the world's largest **coral** reef. It
lies in the Coral Sea, off Australia's northeastern coast.

Coral is made of the skeletons of tiny sea creatures. Hundreds of kinds of coral form the rainbow colors of the reef. Many sea creatures live in and around the reef, including sharks, clownfish, starfish, and angelfish.

▲ *Colorful clownfish swim near coral animals called giant anemones.*

▲ A diver inspects a large red whip coral in the Great Barrier Reef.

The Great Barrier Reef is a popular spot for
Australians and visitors from other countries. People
like to dive, snorkel, and sail there.

The Future of Australia

In the 1960s, Australia changed its law about who could come to Australia to live. The new law allowed many more non-European immigrants into the country. Today, Australians are a rich mixture of people from many countries. Many come from nearby Asia.

▲ These Australian children come from Greek, Maori, Aborigine, and Vietnamese families.

People from all over the world come to visit
Australia too. Australians are proud that their country
was chosen to host the 2000 Summer Olympics in
Sydney. Hundreds of thousands of sports lovers and
athletes filled the city for several weeks in September
2000. Some Australians think tourism is good for

▲ Aborigine children from the Walpiri tribe from central Australia

Australia. Others worry that too many visitors could hurt certain areas of the environment.

If you visit Australia, you will probably learn more about this unusual continent. Then as you leave, you might say, "Thanks, mate. I like the Land Down Under!"

Glossary

Aborigines—the first Australians

boomerang—a curved wooden stick that comes back to the thrower

continent—one of Earth's seven great landmasses

coral—skeletons of tiny sea creatures

dingo—a wild dog

equator—an imaginary line around the middle of the Earth

marsupial—an animal that carries its young in a pouch on its stomach

outback—rugged land in the center of Australia

plains—flat land

plateau—high, flat land with steep sides and a flat top

Did You Know?

- Kangaroos can jump as far as 6 feet (2 meters) in a single leap.

- The wooden trumpet called a didjeridoo is made from a eucalyptus branch hollowed out by termites.

- Australia produces more wool than any other country.

- The Aborigines painted wonderful designs on rocks and tree bark.

At a Glance

Official name: Commonwealth of Australia

Capital: Canberra

Official language(s): English

National song: "Advance Australia Fair"

Area: 2,978,147 square miles
(7,713,364 square kilometers)

Highest point: Mount Kosciusko, 7,310 feet (2,230 meters) above
sea level

Lowest point: Lake Eyre, 52 feet (16 meters) below sea level

Population: 18,613,087 (1998 estimate)

Head of government: Prime minister

Money: Australian dollar

Important Dates

1600s   European explorers visit Australia.

1770   Captain James Cook claims eastern Australia for Great Britain.

1788   Captain Arthur Phillip brings prisoners to Australia and builds the first British settlement.

1700s– 1800s   Many Aborigines die from disease, war, or mistreatment by European settlers.

1850   The British government stops sending prisoners to Australia.

1851   Gold is discovered in New South Wales and Victoria.

1901   Australia becomes an independent country.

1960s   Australia changes its immigration laws.

1967   A new law returns some land to Aboriginal people.

1993   Sydney is chosen as the site of the 2000 Summer Olympics.

Want to Know More?

At the Library

Browne, Rollo, and Chris Fairclough (photographer). *A Family in Australia*. Minneapolis: Lerner, 1987.

Darian-Smith, Kate. *Exploration into Australia*. Parsippany, N.J.: New Discovery Books, 1996.

Lowe, David, and Andrea Shimmen. *Australia*. Austin, Tex.: Raintree Steck-Vaughn, 1997.

On the Web

Australia Downunder
http://library.thinkquest.org/28994/index.html
For information about Aboriginal and modern history, Australian animals, places to visit, famous people, government, and geography

Zoom School: Australia
http://www.zoomschool.com/school/Australia/
For information about Australia's folk music, animals, art, and stories

Through the Mail

Embassy of Australia
1601 Massachusetts Avenue, N.W.
Washington, DC 20036
For information about Australia

On the Road

Australian Travel Information
180 North Michigan Avenue
Chicago, IL 60601
312/368-0525
To find out about visiting Australia

Index

About the Author

Shirley W. Gray received her bachelor's degree in education from the University of Mississippi and her master's degree in technical writing from the University of Arkansas. She teaches writing and works as a scientific writer and editor. Shirley W. Gray lives with her husband and two sons in Little Rock, Arkansas.